WHOSE ARE *You?*

WHOSE ARE You?

Whose will you be on the last day?

Awakening to the Great Reality

— JAMES BARS —

ISBN: 978-0-9817534-0-9

Second Edition Published by Home Of Love Publicationss 2012

Editor: Blake Bars
Cover Design: Nathaniel Taintor - Golden Apples Design
Interior Layout: Blake Bars, Nathaniel Taintor - Golden Apples Design

DEDICATION

This journey is dedicated to you.

May the light that reflects from these pages warm your soul and brighten the horizons of your eternal destiny.

Ten percent of author proceeds from the sale of all James Bars' books are divided equally among the following charities.

Water for People

Child Fund International

ADRA

Compassion International

World Vision

Please join us in providing for the needs of God's children around the world. Select a charity and give. Give of yourself and you will find joy. Jesus said that when we do things for His children in need, it is as if we were doing them for Him. Let us store our treasures in Heaven.

I HOPE YOU DANCE!

Lee Ann Womack, the voice of an angel, delivers a critical prayer in the song written by Tia Sillers and Mark Sanders. "I Hope You Dance." The song was written during a painful time in Tia's life as she came to realize that she would survive.

The first few verses of this poetic masterpiece have been quoted below. They are a hope filled invitation to you.

"I hope you never lose your sense of wonder.
You get your fill to eat, but always keep that hunger.
May you never take one single breath for granted.
God forbid, love ever leave you empty-handed.

I hope you still feel small when you stand beside the ocean.
Whenever one door closes, I hope one more opens.
Promise me that you'll give faith a fighting chance.
And when you get the choice to sit it out or dance.

I hope you Dance.
I hope you Dance."

Don't be a wallflower in the dance of life. Enlarge, develop, discover, release the pain, live, laugh, love, choose joy, dance!

You are a masterpiece of symmetry and design, of emotions and challenge, of striving and hope, of beauty and desire.

As you wrestle with the struggles of life displayed on the pages of this power-bound work, it is our earnest hope that you will become increasingly awakened to the reality of not only who you are but *whose* you are and join us in this beautiful dance of life.

May He awaken you,
James Bars

"Come to me, all you who are weary and burdened, and I will give you rest. Take my yoke upon you and learn from me, for I am gentle and humble in heart, and you will find rest for your souls." Matthew 11:28-29 NIV

TABLE OF CONTENTS

Chapter One

Who Am I?

An identity crisis is the feeling of confusion and despair caused by the lack of knowing who we are and where we fit in the scheme of things. The term was coined by Erik Erikson (1902 – 1994), a psychologist who was instrumental in forming the theory of social development.

Who am I? The answer to this question, we all seek.

In the original movie Wall Street, Bud Fox was the culpable young stock broker. Bud found himself asking what he thought was the question of questions as he awakened in the deep of the night, uncomfortable, empty and lost in his posh New York City apartment. He had sacrificed his personal integrity and sold his soul in the pursuit of wealth. Did he have it made? He had gathered riches beyond his wildest expectations. He had the woman he had longed for. He was living in luxury. Yet when all he thought he wanted was his, he still suffered the anxious pangs of a hollow soul. He awakened in the night, stood on his balcony overlooking the city and asked in bewilderment, "Who am I?"

How many of us have pondered this same question? How many of us have endured or are still enduring our own personal identity crises?

Who am I?

We all have a name here on earth. We have many roles we play. We are sons and daughters. We are sisters and brothers. We are fathers and mothers. We are husbands and wives. We are employees and employers. We are business owners, writers, artists, truck drivers, soldiers, doormen, janitors, chief executive officers, street children, prisoners, board members, thieves, police officers and we fill a myriad of other roles and occupations. But these are things that we do, positions that we hold and our relationship to others—they are not who we are.

Where can we go to discover who we are? We may search for identity in our homeland. "I'm American." "I'm Irish." "I'm African." "I'm Hispanic, Chinese or German." "I'm Scottish-Polish-Native American on my father's side and my mother was Jewish." But this is simply our ethnicity or heritage.

We may search for our identity in an organization, cultural phenomenon or group of some type. "I'm a Veteran of Foreign Wars." "I'm a member of the Rotary." "I'm a Methodist." "I'm a Catholic." "I'm a Seventh Day Adventist." "I'm an atheist." "I'm a Baptist." "I am an Oregon Ducks fan, an Avril Lavigne fan, or a Rolling Stones fan." Yet these are simply groups of people we associate ourselves with—they do not define us.

Perhaps we will seek our identity through a disease or physical impairment, "I am an addict." "I am fat." "I am skinny." "I am hot." I am ugly." "I am crippled." "I am a diabetic, a cancer survivor, a heart patient or dyslexic." But this is not who we are.

Many of us struggle to find our identity through our careers or our material possessions. It seems that many of us believe we are what we do, we are what we own or it is a combination of these that somehow defines us. Many cultures hold this opinion. Perhaps some of us have, from time to time, cast aside our personal freedoms, our joys, our families, our faith, even our physical well-being in mad pursuit of this bewildering phenomenon. We thought we would find ourselves in a title, in fame and/or fortune. Our culture, our parents, our friends—everyone harmonized in this song of distraction. The dominant tune of the identity seekers chorus seems to repeat this overriding refrain—*"Who I am, is revealed by what I do, what I own and how I look."* Our title, possessions and physical appearance *must* define who we are. This *has to* be true, because so many believe it and demonstrate it through their actions.

In light of this apparent truth, we surrender our entire life building identity through material acquisition and outward appearance. We do the things, have the stuff and look the way that fits with who we think we are. It makes sense, doesn't it?

Many of us are enslaved by our careers, possessions and appearances. We work hard to pay the mountain of debt we incur in an attempt to identify ourselves by living in the proper houses in the proper neighborhoods, driving the proper cars, wearing the proper clothes, the proper earrings, even the proper hairstyle. We eat at the proper restaurants. We seek to know the proper people. It all must fit with who believe we are. We *must certainly* be defined by what we own, by what we wear, by where we eat, by who we know, by what we do, by who we are married to and/or the size of our bank accounts. That's got to be it! Right?

If I am a very successful business person I may echo statements like these: *"I must wear only Gucci and Yves Saint Laurent. I can't wait until the new Mercedez is available, my next one will definitely be red, the white one just doesn't stand out in a crowd.*

If my house is not at least 8,000 square feet—well I am just not quite there yet. You simply must go to my stylist, darling! She is to die for!"

If I am a rancher, with a 2,000 head cow/calf operation—an ol' cowpoke, you may hear me say: *"Just the finest horse and buggy for me partner. Gimme them there Wranglers. Where's my danged ol' horse? We gotta take first place at the fair this year pumpkin. Where's my Garth Brooks CD? Git in the truck darlin', we're a headin' in ta town!"*

If I am an old hippie you may hear me rap like this man: *"I am for peace and free love, man. Don't give your life to the machine, man. Why don't we do it in the road? Make love not war, man. Where did I put my tie-died t-shirt, man? My flip flops? My keys? My van? Have you seen my ol' lady, man? Whoa, that's some dynamite hash, maaaaan! Far out, man!"*

These may seem true. Yet they're not really me, and they're not really you.

These may simply be mind-numbing distractions. Perhaps they are designed to keep us from focusing on the Great Reality. Could they possibly be intended to entice us away from a deeper question? Could they be drawing us away from a more relevant wondering?

Consider this—what if our dilemma is that we are not even asking the right question?

What if the truly consonant question that has been lingering deep within the turbulence of our struggling hearts, hidden from all prying eyes, including our own—what if the most pertinent question we need to answer is not, "Who am I?"

What if the deepest question, the ultimate question, the question's answer that will complete us, is not "Who am I?" But, "Whose am I?"

Chapter Two

Whose Am I?

"What?"

"What do you mean, *whose* am I?"

Hold on. We will explain.

But, we must embark on a journey to discover the answer to this vital question.

This…crucial question.

We must leave our little homes, our little jobs, our little titles and our little towns. We are must leave our little country, our little planet, even our little solar system. We shall venture past our galaxy. We will travel far into the secret scenes of the past, the present and the future. We will journey into the depths of our most earnest wonderings.

During our fascinating adventure we will travel deep into the very heart and soul of all creation. We shall seek and we shall find the *Desire of Ages*.

We will set our minds to gain understanding, we will discard any cherished blindness and allow our hearts to draw us into a voyage across the infinite expanse of life. We will lay down our guard and expose ourselves to the majestic winds of the Spirit of the universe. We will set sail toward the shores of our eternal destiny.

There will be a series of critical, life enhancing, enlightening discoveries. We shall stay aware as we seek the Way, the Truth and the Life.

We will battle against our pre-conceived notions and beliefs.

We must be willing to open our hearts and let the truth that is there flow into our minds. We must take our sights off our perceived place on this tiny speck of dust we live on, at the edge of our, one-in-a hundred billion or more galaxies.

Let us breakdown the dark doors that have locked us in the shadows and bound us to slavery. We must tear off the blinding vail of deceit that limits us to nearsighted vision and narrow minded, temporary aspirations.

We will be set free from the shackles and bonds of limited thinking and grow ever toward the Son-light of our true home.

As you are aware by now—life here, on planet earth, is a very temporary experience. This place is not our home. It is a dark room where negatives are developed. It is a quarantined world. It is a desert of testing. It is a valley of decision. It is a rung on the ladder toward fulfillment—toward home. We will open the gate and return to the garden.

The day is dawning, let us awaken to its rapid approach!

Right now, there are billions of fellow travelers on this rapidly moving third rock from the sun. Most, spend little if any of their precious few moments here considering what is next. Many are under the delusion that our existence is by chance—a result of an explosion of some fantastic magnitude. Many souls who are now awake, once suffered from this limiting mental justification; it is an easy means of denying our true hearts calling. However, this particular mental construct and fabrication, grasped by those seeking to find comfort in doing what feels good, while forgoing the blatant reality of their true consciousness is easily disproved. We simply need to take the time to investigate with our hearts open to the True Voice.

There is too much precise immutable law at work on our planet, in our galaxy and throughout the vast seemingly limitless universe—too much interdependence—too much evidence of intelligent design—too many wonderful coincidences that shout, "Glorious creation!"

Whether you are a believer, re-believer or pre-believer, you may want to pause. Take a breath. Relax.

Stop running for a moment. Look around—really look. See beyond your limited mind set. Listen to that still small voice that echoes within. Listen to the rhythm of life. Hear the symphony that surrounds you. Open the eyes of your heart.[1] They long for a vision beyond the short struggle we are now living. Lift the eyes of your heart upward.

What if we are not human beings having a spiritual experience? What if we are spiritual beings having a human experience?

Awaken![2]

Throughout this book we will refer to the One who made all things, as Jesus, the Creator and/or the Son of God. Don't run away. If you are currently a person who is searching, you may have pondered many of the questions that follow.

Is there actually a Creator God out there somewhere? Is there life outside our little planet? Is Jesus our Creator? Is there an afterlife? Is there a day of reckoning? Am I going to be held accountable for my life's choices, thoughts and actions? Are you serious?

Don't close the door of understanding. Breathe in life—dispel the darkness. His story resides inside you. It dwells in every cell of your being and you know it. Stop shutting down. We will lift off toward the realm of reality. We want you on the journey with us. We are heading home.

But, you may hesitate, you may say to yourself - *"I am too intelligent. I am too successful. I am comfortable with my little vision. The football game is on."* Any excuse will be enough for you if you want out—if you can't grow—if you don't want to know—if you close your mind and harden your heart.

You may cancel your flight. You may resist the light.

The Creator desperately wants you to travel to Him, but He will acknowledge your most precious and regal right—your freewill power of choice.

You do choose. You will choose to walk down the short, limited path toward your final day of existence—the path of darkness—the path that dead ends—the path toward your extinction; or you will choose the light and awaken to the reality of our Creator God, His love for us and His gift of eternal joy.

It is a conscious choice to open your ears to hear, your eyes to see, your mind to know and your heart to understand the truth about who you are and whose you are. You must make the choice to embark on a spiritual journey and discover the answers to life's most pertinent questions.

We have chosen to pursue the quest. We will travel to the abode of light.[3]

Will you join us on our journey?

Chapter Three

A Galaxy Far, Far Away

Yes!

Excellent!

You decided to stay with us!

Sweet!

You are free to leave at anytime, but please, don't.

Our journey is not a new one, billions of souls have made the trip before us. It is a supernatural journey of vision. As with nearly every initiative it will involve the elements of commitment, faith, hope, trust, desire and willingness. It is always right to investigate. But don't surrender your inborn desire to travel down this path simply because it doesn't fit into the borders of your current library of knowledge. Allow for new horizons. Insight is a gift, be open to receive it.

This journey may evoke many uncomfortable conflicts. You may feel at times like you are in the midst of a raging battle, it is because you are. It is a battle for you. A battle for that part of you designed to live on beyond this earthly struggle. The soul of you. The heart of you. As we draw near to the end of our story, the warfare may increase. There are two forces contending for the right to call you home. One wants your end, one wants your beginning. You do choose, whose you are. Indecision is a choice.

Let us board our travel craft. It is time.

Baam! We are instantly transported across the universe to the place of unquenchable bliss, to the place of perfection, peace and unbridled joy. We find ourselves in the abode of light.[1] We have come to the inner chamber of the throne room of God. He dwells in unfathomable light. He radiates with the power of thousands upon thousands of suns. He is light and love.[2] The core of His being is light and truth and love. When he speaks creation appears. We collapse in His presence, not from fear but from a heart overflowing with the sheer magnitude of His glory. We experience a sense of belonging and home. This sensation envelopes us in a cocoon of warmth and peace.

"Wait a minute, this is too much!"

"Are you serious?"

"I can't buy this!"

"Are you asking me to believe that this is true? Do you expect me to believe that there is some kind of Creator God out there somewhere?"

"Gimme a break!"

This is good. You are using your brain. We want your intelligence to be involved in this experience. We want your very best consideration and most intense focus during our journey. Engage your brain, utilize the best of your intelligence, but don't forget that this is a journey of the heart. It is within your heart that you decide whose you are.

You will discover as you awaken that this story is not new to you. It has been programmed into the very essence of your DNA. It is the true battle between good and evil. Why do you think that nearly every movie and every novel contain the following basic ingredients—good guys, bad guys and the battle. The good guys don't always win, but we always feel better when they do. This conflict between good and evil is hard-wired into the very fabric of our beings.

If you are a pre-believer, don't be surprised when you want to run and hide from the truth. Don't feel concerned when every part of you feels drawn and compelled to rip this book into little pieces and go back to sleep. You may feel that way because these topics may cut into a place inside you that you wish to defend. It is our nature to resist the light. We were born to a broken, rebellious race.

This has been overcome. We can be reborn! We can be awakened to life! Awakened to the story! At this very moment, you are living right smack in the middle of it! Stay alert! Don't let the thief break into your house and take what is rightfully yours!

Travel with us into our Creator God's throne room. . .

It is alive with the sounds of thousands upon tens of thousands of light-based beings, singing together in perfect harmony. They are enraptured in a chorus of joy so inspiring that we find ourselves lifted up and drawn into the thrill of their absolute exuberance and passion. Tears flow from our eyes as we are raised to heights of understanding and acceptance that illicit from us an urgent, burning desire to draw closer to Him. We want to run to Him because we know that He knows. He knows! He feels! We suddenly realize that He has been with us since before we began. He is the one who sooths our souls through the pain, through the loss, through the emptiness that we endure.

He was there when we had everything we thought would fulfill us, but still felt empty. He knew our every desire, our every thought our every deed whether base or beautiful. We are swept away as we realize that He has chosen not to remember our ugliness. He has chosen only to recall His love for us. We have finally found the Way to fill the gnawing, hungry hole in our soul. We are filled with abundant love, penetrating peace and jubilation as joy pours from us with every tear. We kneel before the *Desire of Ages*. We are home.

The room is immeasurable! The ceiling must be miles off the floor. We can't see the end of it in any direction. As we spin to capture the immensity of this magnificent place we are amazed at the vibrancy of life pouring from every being. There is perfection in the harmonious song and action of them together. It is like seeing a flock of birds all moving in synchronized perfection. How can they all know when to move at exactly the same time? It is as if they are one. We are drawn in. Every fiber of our being wants in. This is it! This is what our souls have longed for! Completeness!

As we move closer to the throne of God we notice that there is a river flowing from it. The River of Life. Beside the River is the Tree of Life and the Garden. The Garden of Eden.[3]

Beautiful!

The streets are paved with pure gold.[4] Every being projects a spirit of welcome. It's as if they have been waiting in anticipation for us. We want to belong. We want to join in. We wish to stay. Then we remember that we are just visiting. We are still members of the family of man—the offspring born in rebellion. We are heart-broken with the knowledge that we will need to travel back to earth and complete our time there. Complete our mission. With heavy hearts we stand—watching—listening.

We are summoned to the throne. Without fear or anxiety, comfortable with the knowledge and understanding of our place, we move forward toward them. We notice two thrones. The Father sits upon the main throne and the Son sits upon a throne to his right.[5] They are not beings of flesh and blood. They are beings of light. Love radiates with every beam. We are immobilized at the air of nobility and wisdom that surrounds their presence.

The Father speaks: "Come sons and daughters of man. We have given you all that you need for life. We have opened the door to knowledge, wisdom and understanding.[6] You have been given the keys to the kingdom.[7] Your hearts and minds have been awakened. Now we must reveal to you the tragic tale of disloyalty, of disobedience, of pride, of self. You will know the truth and the truth shall make you free.[8] To him who has ears to hear and eyes to see—let him know.[9] To him who won't know—let him go."[10, 11]

"You will be shown the seeds of death, discord, and darkness. This knowledge will open your hearts to the war. You will be given peace in the midst of the conflict.[12] You will discover the Way out of the darkness back to the realm of love and light."

"Stay on the marked path. Keep your eyes, ears and hearts open. Hear truth, see life, feel love. You will know them—each one."

"Come my children let us begin."

Chapter Four

Into the Heart of Darkness

Exposing fraud is often a difficult endeavor. If it could be easily seen it wouldn't be so easily used to deceive intelligent beings. Have you ever been to a magic show? Things seem to happen that you know can't happen. But they appear real. Have you ever been disappointed by someone you trusted? Someone who placed their own needs above yours. Someone that led you to believe that he or she was looking out for you but as it turned out, their true motive was to get only what they wanted regardless of how you were affected?

We have a great deceiver in our midst! His name you know. His lies you have experienced. His pain you have felt. His deceptions have crushed the light and life out of many beautiful souls. His purpose is to destroy. To kill, to steal and to destroy.[1]

He was the most honored created being in the courts of the Father's government. He stood in the presence of the thrones of the Father and the Son. His name meant "Light Bearer or Morning Star."[2] He was dubbed, "Lucifer."

He walked in nobility of character. He was admired, trusted, loved. His beauty was above all other created beings in the kingdom. His rank among the inhabitants in the home of perfect bliss was—chief above all. He was placed above all except the Father and the Son. Lucifer was made, perfect![3]

Before he chose to travel down the path of duplicity, all beings were vibrant and alive as they operated in unison under the simple, right and true laws of the kingdom of light. Throughout the entire universe there did not exist any discord. Every being operated in sweet harmony, uninterrupted peace, security, safety and love. There was no lack, no loss. A symphony of light and love shone through each and every being as the life enhancing music of our Creator God vibrated in all and through all.

This universe was built upon the sure foundation of love, for the Father is love. His every thought and action is born from love. Love can only flourish in an atmosphere of absolute freedom. It cannot be coerced. It cannot be demanded. It cannot be purchased. It can only be given freely.

It is because of their great love that the Father and the Son established the laws of love and bestowed upon every created being the right to freely obey or reject the guiding principles of their kingdom.

Every kingdom, every nation, every family, every organization of any kind has its laws, its rules, its expectations, its rights of membership.

The right to belong freely to any organization is granted as long as one is willing to abide by the laws of that organization. Laws are generally established to allow the members of an organization to operate in a known, safe environment. They are designed to ensure the survival of each individual and the organization as a whole.

Without law there is no harmony, no freedom, no safety, no security, no foundation, no trust.

When a father warns his child to stay away from a fire, he does this out of love and concern for the safety of his child, not to restrict or withhold anything good from his loved one. He knows that if his precious, innocent child falls into the fire, he will suffer. The child will suffer and the father will suffer also, because the father's heart of love wants the best for his baby. He longs to protect him from any harm, damage, loss or grief. He desires only joy, safety, peace and happiness for his sweet, darling.

Any loving, responsible father will create a body of rules for his children. A government will do the same thing for its people.

The Father and the Son were the first to do this. They diligently designed and established the laws of love to protect and enhance the lives of their children. The laws of the Father's kingdom are the laws of love. When all operate within these laws, there is peace, safety, growth, contentment, trust, guaranteed freedom, and harmony. When the law is broken, there is fear, uncertainty, discord, discontentment, distrust and unbridled bondage.

Harmony in the kingdom of light was lost. It was lost when the great rebel, Lucifer, chose to violate the laws of love.

How could this happen?

Self-centered pride is where it all began.

His dark rebellion began with a subtle admiration of himself.

He was the most exalted among all created beings. He was beautiful beyond description, perfect in all aspects of his being. Intelligent above all others except the Father and the Son. He had charge over the countless inhabitants of the kingdom. He stood beside the throne of God.

He was God's gift!

But he fell from the heights of heaven to the depths as the most disgusting and vile creature in all creation. All because he lost sight of . . . whose he was. He lost the vision. His heart traveled inward toward self and far from the sure Way of love. He desired to place his throne above the Father's and above the throne of the One who gave him life—the Creator. Pride may be the most insidious offense among all of the ways to violate the heart of God's vision for His children.

It seems pride can find a way to justify any dark thought or action. All selfishness can be traced back to this most dangerous vacuum, this sink hole, this backwater eddy where life is sucked away and love is drowned.

Lucifer is the father of lies. They all began with pride. He no longer wished to bring glory to the Father and the Son. He wanted it for himself. He said in his dark heart. "I will place my throne above all thrones. I will be like the Most High." His desire was to usurp the Father and the Son.[4]

His heart of darkness would no longer subject itself to the light of love. He turned away.

Many of the other perfect inhabitants of the kingdom of light pleaded with him to come back. The Creator sought him out and attempted to illuminate him with the truth—he wouldn't listen. These actions only caused Lucifer to commit more allegiance to himself and his black path. He had one last chance to withdraw from this terrible pit, yet pride would not allow him to retreat. His course was set. His mastermind was locked firmly against the truth. He would have it all or he would have nothing.

He will have nothing.[5] As we all know—good will always triumph over evil.[6, 7, 8] Love never fails.[9]

The story was told before it began. There is nothing better for all created beings than what the Father has freely provided.

He knows all.

The selfish heart is deceitful above everything.[10] Denial of truth, cultivation of pride, justification, rationalization, greed, hatred, lust, envy—these fruits are produced when a soul severs the cords of love.

War, destruction, heartbreak, misery, monotony, emptiness, tears, death—these are a few of the end results of prideful rebellion against the Father and His beautiful laws of love.

Chapter Five

The War Begins

Propaganda: It was born in the soul of greed. It is a twisted, mind numbing confusion designed to unsettle innocent hearts. It is used to deliver allegations against one's enemy. To sway hearts and minds into believing a lie. To pervert the truth. To win over. To create fear. It is often used to distract, to undermine, to subdue, to divert, to subvert. Used properly it can win a battle before it even begins. This would become the tool used by the great deceiver to turn the hearts embraced in love away from allegiance to the Father and the Son.[1]

Before the controversy became overbearingly confusing, the Father summoned all angels into His presence and presented the truth before them in order that informed decisions could be made. The great deceiver twisted and perverted the truth to build his allegations against the Father. However, the Father can only be who He is truth, love and light.

The Father gives freewill and intelligence to his dearly loved children. His heart of love desires a willing allegiance; he will not ask for any heart that is not freely offered.

The most precious gift the Father and the Son could have possibly offered to their created beings was and is freedom. True freedom within the kingdom of light can only exist inside the framework of the laws of love.

The distortion of the intent behind these laws was the weapon that the first rebel, Lucifer, used to bring chaos to God's kingdom of light. Using deceit, outright lies and duplicity in a vain effort to overthrow the kingdom, he shattered the fabric of peace that had enveloped each trusting heart.

The kingdom of light and the kingdom of darkness are separated by this one most significant factor—freewill.

The kingdom of darkness binds beings in slavery.

The kingdom of light offers absolute freedom to all.

Lucifer would infer that there was no need for the inhabitants of the kingdom of light to have laws enforced upon them. Are angels not perfect already? He would attempt to lead them to believe that these laws were designed to manipulate and control them. He would insinuate that the Father and the Son were withholding from them a higher level of attainment. He would try to destroy trust in the laws of love by implying that they were designed to hold the created beings back from greater and greater achievements and accomplishments. He strived to instill the belief that the laws were being used to diminish the created beings and to pridefully exalt the Father and the Son. His deception was delivered in such a way that many were lead to distrust God. Lucifer was subtle, beguiling and relentless in his campaign of lies. He proposed a lawless society, a supposed state of freedom. But there can be no freedom outside the law.

Any violation of God's law will always bring trouble.[2] It will bring trouble to the one in violation, trouble to those who must enforce the law, trouble to those who have witnessed the violation—trouble to all.[3] This breach of trust that Lucifer gave birth to would trouble every being in the universe. It would send a rippling quake of panic, unprecedented vagary and questioning rumbling into every mind and heart throughout the boundless worlds.

It was a sickening stench. It would be dealt with.

It must be dealt with in a way that would vindicate the Father and the Son, for in order to generate the kind of controversy needed to bring angels of the light into his dark realm, Lucifer would need to put God on trial.[4] He would accuse the Father and the Son of forcing the allegiance of all beings into compliance to their laws. He would point to the laws of love as a violation of their rights and privileges. He would distort their intent and cause disaffection through propaganda, lies, distrust, flattery, any undermining means he could create and circulate from his mastermind of twisted, pulsing darkness.

He became something heretofore unknown in all creation. He became scared. Fear began to envelope him. He liked it.

The Father and the Son walk in faith. The enemy walks in fear. All power is from God. The enemy can only use us to distort God's power and bend it to his use. This he achieved.

Faith and fear will bring into reality that which each seeks. This enemy of truth, Lucifer, must try to appear as if he were contending for what was best for the other created beings. All the while he weaved his sophistry into the fabric of peace that he sought to shatter for his own benefit and no one else's. He was allowed to proceed on his course, for if the Father and the Son were to destroy him before the true essence of his desires were revealed, those who remained loyal to them might do so out of fear rather than love. Love and fear cannot coexist.

So Lucifer worked slyly to gain the confidence of the angels of light. He felt that if he could mislead those that dwelt in the very presence of the Father and of the Son, then those that dwelt on the outer worlds would also join him in overthrowing the kingdom of light.

All of those that joined Lucifer's rebellion were given constant opportunity to return to their previous state of peace, until the situation grew into open rebellion. Once the prince of darkness escalated his cause to the level of blatant disregard for the safety of those who remained loyal to the Father and the Son, then action needed to be taken to protect the remnant of the kingdom of light.[5]

It was a sad day in the heart of the Father. Lucifer, the most honored and privileged of all created beings in the kingdom must be torn from the land and cast out with the train of rebels that he had gathered. Grief struck deep into the very core of the Great Parent that day as He ordered the angels he loved, banished from their home.

Pain and loss wait at the end of all selfish ambition.

The rebels would be banished and quarantined in the outer reaches of the Father's realm, where Lucifer, now stripped of his title and position, would become known as Satan. Here he would be allowed to exercise the tenants of his government to all beings. A government built upon open rebellion against the Father and on rejection of His laws of love. Satan would begin a fear based, kingdom of bondage.[6]

It was a devastating, heart-breaking battle, wounding all that were left behind and all that were cast out.

Chapter Six

Enter the Spirit

Prior to the war in the kingdom of light plans had been formulated to create and add an entirely new galaxy to God's universe. As a part of this new endeavor, a small solar system would be included. In this new system, the heart of life would dwell on the planet called Earth.

Before the Father and the Son advanced upon this endeavor they sent themselves ahead to begin preparation.[1]

"What? They sent themselves ahead? How did they do that?"

They are one. One in purpose. One in power. One in thought. They pervade every strand of DNA that they have ever designed. But they are not alone. There is a third member of their existence. His name is Spirit. He, like them, is all and is in all.[2, 3]

As the Father and the Son began preparations for the beginning of this new expansion, He was joined by them and the miracle was underway. It would take seven days from evening to evening each day to complete the project.

They had performed this creative process billions of times before in bringing forth other galaxies and solar systems. The task that seemed beyond belief, they had perfected. The most elaborate systems would come together precisely in the most effective life generating, life sustaining way. The most powerful source of life energy available—faith—would be used in the birthing process. All would be accomplished through the force of faith. They would speak each and every life form into being. They would call things that are not as though they were, and they would be.[4]

"In the beginning was the Word, and the Word was with God, and the Word was God. He was with God in the beginning. Through him all things were made; without him nothing was made that has been made. In Him was life, and that life was the light of all mankind."[14]

The word of life spoke, and . . .

Colors, systems, sub-systems, cell types, the elements, the breath of life ingredient, timing, flesh tones, water content, interdependencies, habitats, molecule designs and functions, power sources, reproductive systems, instincts, sight receptors, hearing receptors, touch receptors, smell receptors, taste receptors, watering systems, light refraction, distances, shapes, waste recycling, bacteria's, immune systems, moons, stars, densities of matter, temperatures, depths, flight patterns, emotional abilities, vocal chords, communication systems, time, evaporation rates, gravitational levels, speeds of light and sound, oxygen producers, carbon dioxide producers, adaptation abilities, mental functions, hair follicles, lung capacities, trillions upon trillions of simultaneous decisions and actions occurring nearly instantaneously.

Beautiful!

The knowledge of our Creator God can be clearly seen, being understood from what has been made, so that men are without excuse.[5]

The title of "Creator" encompasses more than our limited understanding can begin to fathom. Maybe we can understand the formation of a molecule, but what gives it life?

Only the Father, the Son and the Spirit can explain.

We were brought forth by the Voice of love. Awe generating, unquenchable love. Our perfect planet sits within a galaxy so immense that it would take 330 million years for it to make one revolution and it is only one of billions upon billions of galaxies, each one brought forth by our Creator God.

On the sixth day of creation, man was formed from the dust of the earth and was given the breath of life.[13]

Man was placed in charge of the planet. He was given authority over everything upon the earth.[6] He was granted free access to the Father and communicated with the angels of light that traveled from home to here. He was perfect in every aspect. Also bestowed upon him was his most treasured possession and gift—freewill.

The Father's heart can only love. He is love. Love may exist only when freely given. So man was given the freedom to accept the very best or to walk away. Beaming with intelligence and perfection of character there did not exist within him any desire to violate the laws of love. He understood the generosity of his Creator and did not wish to separate himself from His love, power and beautiful presence.

Into this spotless, new, gleaming world came the enemy.[7]

The Father had placed one limitation upon man as a test of fidelity. He informed him that he must not eat the fruit of the tree of knowledge of good and evil, else he would surely die.[8]

This, the enemy would place his focus on and use to entice man to distrust the One he loved.[9] Devastating, rip tides of loss and pain would stream from man's decision to believe the conspiring propaganda delivered from the smooth lips of the enemy of souls. Man would lose his home, and the privilege of direct face to face communion with the Father and the Son.

Weeping, man was driven from his Eden home, stripped of his covering of light he knew nakedness for the first time and was now dressed in the skin of the first dead creature.[10] He was wearing the hide of a creature that he had loved, a creature that he had named and played with. Now all other creatures shied away from him.

He was crushed. He was changed. Something was inherently different. He had turned to the dark side. A previously unknown enemy now resided within him. He longed to go back. He wished to reverse his decision. "Please Father! I am bowed low in the dirt. I am so, so sorry. Please forgive me and my precious bride. We can't handle all this loss. Oh Father, what have we done?"

But there was no going back. In making his decision to turn away from the truth, he had surrendered his rights. His right to ownership of the planet. His right to unrestricted access to the Father and the Son. His right to live without fear and worry. His right to perfect freedom. He had taken on the yoke of the enemy by giving himself to the dark side.

Oh no!

The evil one rejoiced that he had turned others away from loyalty to the laws of love. Now man was his. He delighted in his cunning ability to use the man's vulnerability with his mate to entice him into violation.[11] It was a dark day, the results of which we live in now. All death and destruction that occurs now as a regular event in our beautiful world streams from that choice. "Way to go Adam. What a dufus. I certainly wouldn't have chosen your path. Or would I? Or have I? And do I?"

Yes, we all do. For when our earthly father chose death, when he invited the darkness into his soul, he passed it on to his offspring. You know this struggle. You have known it from the day of your first memory. It is a constant battle within your heart. It is the victory and the defeat that you experience in your soul with each and every moment that passes. It arises with every choice that you make.

Paul's words echo this struggle, "So I find this law at work: Although I want to do good, evil is right there with me. For in my inner being I delight in God's law; but I see another law at work in me, waging war against the law of my mind and making me a prisoner of the law of sin at work within me. What a wretched man I am! Who will rescue me from this body of death? Thanks be to God, who delivers me through Jesus Christ our Lord!" [13]

Our first earthly parents, Adam and Eve, took this evil into their hearts and now we are all wired like them. We too will know his heartbreaking loss. We too will surely die. [12] We too will surely grieve, we will know hopelessness and pain and difficulty and uncertainty and confusion. We know the dark side. It colors every decision we make and tempts us to violate the laws of love. But our conscience draws us toward obedience. His Spirit calls us toward the light and we long to live righteous lives. This battle within—this violent tug-of-war between the light and the darkness is our dilemma. We we are born fallen, but we can be reborn to arise - new!

This is the Good News! We have not been left to fend for ourselves.

In their unfailing love, The Father, the Son and the Spirit have given us the Way out of the struggle—the Way up.

Chapter Seven

The Way

Peels of thunder ripped across the tumultuous, mountain skies and shook the tender ground as lightning ignited a near by tree. It exploded, shattering into a rain of dangerous wooden missiles, shooting in all directions. The summer wind pushed hard against the majestic old growth timbers with a life-ending force, causing them to surrender their root bound positions and come crashing to the earth. They call the wind, Mariah. I heard her sing her violent song that day. The storm had come quickly, devastating the area and then—rain. Buckets full! Drenching the forest. Suddenly—the torrential waters poured down all around. Then I heard it. A rumble, at first, like a drum roll, announcing devastation. It came, rapidly tumbling, tearing the narrow gorge I was traversing. Before I could think, it was upon me. A flash flood! A wall of water and mud, bushes, rocks, trees and shrubs. Cascading down upon me, like death. I screamed, "Oh my God!"

That day, those words came as a prayer for salvation. They still do for some, even though they are used as a cute expression today by many people. Those vital words are often spoken without thought. Yet when crises come roaring toward us and we stand helpless, hopeless, powerless—the vision, the reality of those three beautiful words, comes vibrantly alive.

Have you ever wondered why?

Even if we have intellectualized God away. Even after we have chosen to discard the very idea of Him and His existence from our mind. Even after we have joined the church of evolution and given our origins over to the god of pure chance. Even after we have traded Him in for the empty gods of material possessions, food, lust, self, money, chocolate, drugs, power, whatever. Even after we have turned our callous, cold, dead hearts over to the dark side. When crises come thundering down the mountain, threatening to eliminate us from the path of life, that heartfelt, desperate, hopeful prayer - "Oh my God" - is often the cry of our fearful hearts.

I didn't know why. I do now. Now I face a different flood. A flood of life. A flood of love. A flood filled with hope and future. A flood that lifts up and inspires. A beautiful torrent of light, carrying me away to higher and higher, awe-evoking visions of Him.

"Oh my God!"

I often just sit gazing at his beauty in something or someone that He has created and suddenly I am aware of the freshness of life, of the impossibility of life, of the fascinating reality of life and I wonder: "How is it that He chose me, to awaken?" I was enjoying my evil little habits. My self-focused, narrow, empty-headed, drug-fogged, man-made life style.

Why did He choose to awaken me?

Perhaps, so I could share this story with you. Perhaps, to encourage you if you are searching for home. Perhaps it is because He loves. I know that He loves. I know, because He loves me and I know it. He has made it abundantly clear. He loves to the point of sacrifice. He gives all. He knows no other way. He emptied the treasury of Heaven to ransom me—to ransom you.

This, He has done. The feat is complete. There is a Way out. We have hope. We are not abandoned in this dark world. We need not face certain death, endless death, the second death.[1] We may, if we choose, have a future beyond the grave, beyond the few days that we are trapped on this stage of Satan's aspirations. We have been given the keys of the kingdom.[2] They are deposited in us when we open the door of our rotting hearts and let the healing power of His love enter to lift up, to set us high upon the road to life—the road home.

The Way is open to all who will enter in. The door is wide-open. Let us walk through it and claim our rightful place in the kingdom of light.

To each and every one, He willingly opens his arms, spreads them wide with love and speaks these hopeful words, "Come home."

Let us consider the following relevant parable as we ponder our dilemma.

The judge pronounced his verdict and delivered his final decision upon the young girl as she stood ashamed and trembling before him that day. There was no possible way she could pay the huge fine. She wept. Her head hung low and her shoulders hunched as she sobbed—helpless—guilty as charged. Remorse and fear filled her crushed heart as she faced an unknown end. Then the judge stood up took off his robe, came out from behind the bench, walked down the stairs and approached the court secretary. He took out his wallet. It was filled with his entire life savings. He began to lay down his all to rescue this darling child from the wages of her poor choices.

How could the judge do such a remarkable thing? She had expected him to do what was right because she knew this man. His reputation was flawless. He would uphold the law without fail. He was a champion of right. She felt hope rise in her heart as she realized that he was rescuing her. He was giving up all that he had to save her. Her heart swelled as she watched pure love in action. She willingly accepted the gift as she ran crying into his arms. Tears streaming down her face she looked deep into his eyes of hope and whispered, "Thank you Daddy." She was home, safe, forgiven, free! Yes, the judge was her father. There was only one way he could uphold the law and still save his precious child—he stood in her place and bore her guilt.

Our dilemma is obvious. All we need to do is to look within and simply examine the struggles we encounter in one day or even one hour. The battle for our minds and affections occurs with every breath. In and of ourselves, we are powerless to defeat the enemy of right, the devourer of light.[3]

The good news—he is already defeated! When the Father, the Son and the Spirit laid the foundations of the earth—they knew.

They saw the end from the beginning. They foresaw the choice our first earthly parents would make—to disbelieve God and surrender their souls to the evil one. Adam and Eve fell through the deceit and lies of Satan.

The Father, Son and Spirit had been accused of being unjust. Before the entire universe they faced the charges of Satan and refuted them. They have been acquitted. They have been vindicated.[4] Yet Satan continues to press his unjust, unfounded charges. We are witnesses. We are witnesses for the prosecutor or for the defense, but we are witnesses. We continue to be a witness through every choice we make, whether to surrender to good or to surrender to evil.[5]

As the Father, Son and Spirit considered the fall of man, they were burdened with the need to provide a rescue boat, an ark to safely cross the treacherous waters toward the shores of home. They needed to develop a plan for man—the Way to uphold the laws of love and still give man access to freedom. The Father had no other choice. He would need to bear the burden for man's wrong choice. There is no way man could ever save himself.[6] For to transgress the laws of love, to violate their eternal principles, puts all of creation in danger. The perfect peace of the kingdom of light hinges on all beings living within the safe borders of these laws. The end result of breaking these laws is death.[7] From the day that man turned to the dark side, he perpetuated death for each individual born in this world. From that day to this, the Son has born the burden for every transgression.

It was the Son of God who would become the guilt bearer.[8, 9] He would take upon Himself the entire burden. He would become our substitute. He would empty the treasuries of Heaven. He would willingly offer up everything to save man. He too, had no choice. For love, gives. Love rises up and delivers. Love sets free. Love conquers. There is no greater gift one can give than to lay down his life for his friends.[10] This He would do, with a willing heart. He would sacrifice His most valued treasure—His undivided connection with the Father. For on the day that He would assume the role of guilt bearer, the Father would be separated from Him. This is the life-ending pain that would bring His death.[11] He would die of a broken heart. This is history.

Let's examine the word *history*. Did you ever wonder where the word *history* was born and what its real meaning is. We will tell you. It stands for His-story. All that happens in each brief life born into this troubled world is centered around and will be judged in the light of His-story.

History is chronicled accordingly by dates. All dates are centered around the day that our Creator God came back to earth in form of man. BC stands for Before Christ and AD stands for Anno Domini which is Latin for the Year of our Lord and defines a time period based on the traditionally recognized date of the birth of Jesus of Nazareth. Every time we write a date we acknowledge His story. Not only is His-story the turning point of mankind's physical world chronologically, but it is the climactic moment of our spiritual journey here on earth.

We will discuss His most generous offering on that day, the historical day that He laid all upon the alter of sacrifice. The historical day of perfect and complete victory in the great trial. The historical day when Satan's true desires and the Father's true nature would be revealed for the universe to see. The day the Father's song of grace would be shouted from the rooftops and all would be invited to join in His chorus of love. The human story is camped around this very fire, singing of His glorious mercy and love. Won't you come close, join in and be warmed by its beckoning glow?

Chapter Eight

History

The wild-eyed, brutish, grizzly bear charged, pushing rapidly through the thick brush. He gained with deadly precision upon the innocent child, whose mother was just a few yards away. She had taken her precious, sweet baby into the deep woods on this beautiful, sunny day to pick berries. Her baby loved to pick berries.

Occasionally he would even put one in the basket with Momma's berries, but most of his tasty finds were deposited directly into his berry loving mouth.

She diverted her attention away from him for just a moment as she hummed her favorite song and lifted the delicate leaves to uncover their mouth-watering treasures. As she hummed, she thought about how much her darling husband was going to enjoy today's bountiful discovery. They were plump and juicy and…

A heart searing scream! *Her baby!* "Oh my God!," She screamed, "NO!! NOOOOOOOO!! Oh my God—No!" She lunged toward the roar. Her heart leaped toward her treasured child. "Oh God! Oh God! Oh God!"

Her darling husband grew tired of waiting for them.

"It wasn't like her to be late. Where was dinner?"

Then—the unthinkable thought. His heart sank as he felt it. It came strong. The dark door slammed against his happy life. He felt death envelope him as the hair on his neck stood up.

"Something has gone terribly wrong. They hadn't gone into the deep woods—had they?"

He had warned her to stay away.

"Oh, no."

He found himself running toward the forbidden forest.

"Something is wrong—I told her not to go! Don't go there! I said it—I told her! Oh please, no. They have got to be alright. My son. My baby."

His thoughts raced. His heart thundered against his heaving chest. He sobbed.

"They have got to be okay."

"Honey! Honey!" He cried. "Hooooonnnneeeeyyyyy!" He knew they were gone. Their place in his soul was empty. "Oh Honey No! Don't go!" It was growing darker as he dove deeper and deeper into the blackness. In the twilight he entered the meadow. The beautiful meadow.

He froze.

All was lost.

"Why?"

We are born at war. We are delivered at birth, behind enemy

lines.[1] Our world is the focus of a ravaging war effort. The violations of the laws of love are reaping their horrifying consequences upon all mankind. The universe watches as Satan reveals the effects of his government of darkness upon this stage—planet earth. The Father must allow this enemy to demonstrate the end results of rebellion against the kingdom of light. This must be done so that when this enemy of souls is finally destroyed, every loyal being will understand why and will be enabled to freely enjoy eternal security under the laws of love. They will know that the Father and the Son are right. The story that you know so well will conclude the way you knew it would. Good, will triumph over evil.[2]

However, in the meantime we are still here, facing the terror, the loss, the sadness, the pain of life, in the war of the universe. "This is not fair!" We exclaim. We just want to pick a few berries in the sunlight—in the beautiful meadow. We don't want to be at war. We don't want to be devoured by violence and separation. We don't like this tale of woe. Let's vanish into some other story.

We certainly have the intellectual freedom to decide what we are going to believe. But we cannot deny that place inside us that already knows this story. However, we can stop that calling for our heart; that persistent tugging. We can shut down that still small voice, the one that whispers, "Wake up. The bear is coming!"[3] If we ignore Him long enough, we may no longer hear Him inviting us home.

The Father's heart grieves deeply for each of His children. He desires that none should perish but that all may enter upon the path of life.[4] He longs to rescue us from all the charging grizzly's in this war.

War is messy. Collateral damage rips and shatters every tender heart. All are wounded. The enemy lashes out to kill, to steal and to destroy.[5]

This war was launched by a cunning, ferocious adversary. He has been waging war against the Father and us since He began the great rebellion in heaven. His hatred is fed each time a child of the Father falls prey and dies. He rejoices when our Father stands weeping in a bloody meadow. Weeping over the loss of a precious child. Weeping over the loss of a sweet bride. Will he weep over the loss of us? Yes, unless we choose to avoid the dangers of the deep woods and come home.

When our first, earthly parents surrendered to the dark side, they were infected with a virus. This virus not only damaged their hardware and their software but has been downloaded into each of their offspring.[6] We are by nature, programmed to automatically default toward self.[7] Watch any child, anywhere. They all have the same hard-wired defective drive toward self. This virus spread. It spread the day our first earthly parents surrendered to the enemy. It spread to all living creatures.[8] It is a fatal virus. It is designed to infect and destroy every life it touches.

If you have watched children or even adults, you have certainly heard this: "Mine, mine, mine." We can all act like any two-year-old whose entire focus is on self. All those born on earth are now infected with the with the virus—self.

Did you know that there is enough money in this world right now for every man, woman and child to be a multi-billionaire? Yet nearly thirty thousand children die of malnutrition every day. The United States is touted as the richest nation ever to exist in world history, but nearly ninety percent of the wealth in this country is held by three percent of the population, while the majority of her citizens live paycheck to paycheck.

"Mine, mine, mine," is the mantra of life now on planet earth. It is an infection. Deadly. The silver lining—we have the option to download anti-virus software—free.[10]

We are programmed, through our conscience as well as our

conscious and sub-conscious minds with the ability to connect to the universal internet. Innate within every soul lays this function, this ability to download vital programs that enable us to override the virus. Programs that allow us to delete the infection.[11, 12] Our brain is the single most complex computer design on the planet. Most of us utilize only two to five percent of its functional capacity. Let us open the box and connect with the manufacturers' top of the line input. Let's download the salvation software and give Him full access to our domain.

We are offered, without cost, the Way to re-image our hard drive. This source was provided the day that the Father, the Son and the Spirit laid the foundation of the earth. They knew that man would fall and choose the dark side. They knew all his offspring would be born on the wrong side of the law. They provided pre-paid legal for each soul that would accept the offer. The Son of God became the guilt offering for each soul that would willingly choose His gift. He laid down his rightful place in the kingdom of light and entered this dark realm to bear the burden for man. He provided the Way for us to be ransomed.

We are born in rebellion because of the choice our first earthly parents made. We are born with a selfish nature. But we are also liberated because of the choice our Creator made. We are free. We now belong to Him, if we choose to allow Him to debug our soul.

After man had violated the sacred laws of love and surrendered all of his rights to the dark one, the Father brought to them His plan of reconciliation.[13] The consequence of breaking the law is death. It is like the law of gravity. When you step off of a three thousand foot cliff, without a parachute, you are going to die. Everyone knows that. Our earthly parents Adam and Eve, too, were warned. They would die. Not because the Father is cruel or cold or hard-hearted. It is the result of violating the law.

Satan would have all beings believe that the laws are designed to restrict, control and dominate.[14] Not true. But he is the father of lies and will use any deceitful, heartless, calculating, cold, unremitting falsehood to tear any soul away from the Father, the Son and the Spirit.[15] He is at war. We are at war—like it or not. The Father, Son and Spirit are our shield, our hiding place, our hightower. Our safety in this war lies in surrendered obedience to the great laws of love. We did not choose to be born into this war but we can choose to accept His victory as our own.

We wish to emphasize the fact that the Father, the Son and the Spirit designed the laws to protect and bless. They provide a secure framework under which all created beings in the universe can function and grow. Love and the desire to provide the very best for His children is the Father's intent behind the law.

When the Father, Son and Spirit brought to man the plan of reconciliation, They also provided the best Way for us to access this freedom from rebellion—faith.

Faith is the conductor of creation. It may be likened to electricity. We may not be able to explain exactly how electricity works. But we can turn on a light. We may not be able to explain how faith works. But we can envision something happening with eyes of faith and then watch it come to pass in reality.

When does a pile of rocks cease to be a pile of rocks? The moment a man envisions a cathedral!

This faith power is the best power source available. The Father provides only the best for his children. We were not just born on the wrong side of the law. We were also created in the image and likeness of our Father. To each, there is given a measure of faith. But just like the muscles that cause our body to move on demand will become weak and ineffective without use, so our faith powers will become weak and ineffective without use.

Faith is the substance of things wished for.[16] It is a very real power source. When the Father, the Son and the Spirit speak something into existence, faith is the power that causes the reality to occur. This power source is available to us. It is so powerful that if a person possessed a unit of faith the size of a mustard seed, he could command an entire mountain to move itself and it would be done.[17]

The Father calls things that are not, as though they were, and then they are. When He delivered the plan of reconciliation to man it came with the provision that man needs only to believe it for it to become reality. This is still the offer today. The rights of freedom cannot be earned. They cannot be paid for. They cannot be stolen. They cannot be borrowed. They are free to all through the best, most pure and powerful source available—faith.[18]

Without faith it is not possible to please the Father.[19] He would not deliver inferior or second class provisions of any type to His dearly loved children.

So how do we access this gift? How can we have this faith? How can we experience freedom from the dark one? How can we enjoy victory in the war?

The answer: faith comes by hearing and hearing by the word of the Father, the Son and the Spirit.[20] We need only feed our mind and spirit on the word of God. The more we eat of the word of life, the more weight our faith will bear.

Have you ever been afraid of the dark? Have you ever walked out into a black night and been completely frightened of all of the dark spirits, criminals and monsters lurking there? Has your fear become so real that it caused your heart to race, your breathing to become deeper, your blood pressure to go up and the hair on the back of your neck to stand on end? And then, when you turn on the light, have you discovered that none of it was even there? The dark creatures only existed in your mind—through fear.

Fear is an evil and disabling thread. The fabric of our mind is weaved through and through with this corrosive material.

But it doesn't even exist. The power behind it is actually a perversion of the Father's perfect power of faith. Faith is the substance of things wished for and fear is the substance of things not desired. Focus will bring either about.

Where is our mental and spiritual focus? What are we feeding our minds—our souls? Are we ingesting fear or faith?

When we turn on the light of faith, fear vanishes.

We must exercise our faith muscles through study and practice of the word. We must stop exercising our fear muscles.

Before we continue, we will illuminate the plan of reconciliation the Father determined would most reveal His true character and also provide the most certain and readily available cure for the virus.

It was determined that the Creator would come to earth in the form of a man. He would lay down His royal robes and step down from His rightful throne. He would be born as the Son of Man and the Son of God.[21] He would spend His life in humble toil, as a carpenter, until the day when the Father would send Him forth to announce to all creation that His Son, the Creator, was starting down the path toward that great day when He would become our substitute and would be sacrificed as He bore the sins of the world.[22]

Before His death for us, He would go about demonstrating the power of faith by miraculously healing the sick, raising the dead, foretelling the future, giving sight to the blind and walking on water. He would overcome every evil desire that had been implanted into the heart of man. He would do all of this through the same power that we have available to us—faith.

He would walk in love. His every action, thought, word, look and desire, sprang from the well of love that is the Father's heart. He came to reveal His character to us and to every intelligent being in the universe.

Satan claimed that man could not abide by the laws of love and therefore must be eliminated from existence. The Son of God—our Creator came to illustrate that man can abide by these laws through the power of faith. He was born and lived as a man, yet no blemish stained his perfect character. He laid down His life to fulfill the requirements of the law. He risked it all, for He could have fallen. While here, He was tempted just like we all are to surrender to our nature of self. Yet he did not.[23]

When our first parents stepped off the cliff into the darkness, they brought death to all men. The Son of God came to bring life for each and every one of us.[24] He came to grant us life to the full, here on earth and eternally with Him in heaven.

This He did.

They crucified him. He was nailed to a cross. Death brought about by this tortuous practice was designed by Rome as the most cruel, unprecedented, shameful way to die. It was a long agonizing, painfully slow suffocation. It was done very publicly as a deterrent to those who may consider violating the restrictions placed on them by their Roman rulers.

Rome, the occupying foreign power, used the most fearful, murderous, disheartening butchery to forcefully overwhelm and control the then known world. They were the dominant world power of their day. Into the bloody hands of their most brutal men our Savior placed His weary frame. They ripped the flesh from His body, pierced His bruised and swollen brow with a crown of thorns, drove rough, heavy spikes through His hands and feet, lifted Him high into the air on a wooden cross and slammed it into a narrow hole sending sharp waves of pain tearing through His every quivering nerve and muscle.[25]

Some say that He died from His wounds. But that is not true. For crucifixion was designed to take days to bring the relief of death. Our Savior gave up His Spirit in a matter of hours. He voluntarily surrendered Himself to endure a brutal death on our behalf but He did this with forgiveness in His heart.

The source of His joy, His love, His purpose, His life was His unbroken, perpetual heart's union with the Father.

When he accepted the entire load of guilt for the human race, the Father could not stand in His presence. For goodness and evil cannot coexist. The Father would be forced to withdraw from the Son. This caused His death. It broke His heart. The consequence of violating the law is death. The gift of the Father is life. He provided victory for each soul on that focal, triumphant day of His-story. He was then placed in a tomb and came back to life three days later.[26]
He conquered death, for us![27]

He has granted us all free access to that victory through the most powerful source in existence.[28]

His victory is ours through faith.[29]

He invitingly spreads wide His arms with love and sends this message to all, "Come home."

Chapter Nine

The Valley of Decision

It was likely that I wouldn't return from this mission. It was likely that no one would return from this mission. The night air was a chilling vapor that brushed against my weary soul. Nausea, trembling, an intense desire to run. I wanted to explain to the other members of my 82nd Airborne unit that I really didn't want to do this. I really just wanted to go home.

I thought, *"Why were we doing this anyway? We don't even know these people and here we are trying to kill each other,"*

Death tugged at my arm, again. Nausea, trembling, an intense desire to run.

"I must pray. Where is God anyway? Why would He let this carnage exist if He were such a loving God? I don't want to die! I am so young."

Then the call came, "Mount up men, its time to move out."

"No! Wait! I didn't pray! God! God! What do I say? Forgive me? Accept me? Save me? Do I mean any of this? I should have spent

more time with you. I should know you better. You are my only hope tonight, God!"

"We have little chance of surviving this stupid mission. Why did you put me here? You know I'm not a killer. Maybe I could just slip off and hide until this is over. None of these guys are going to be left alive in a few minutes anyway. How could I live with that? No, I will die with the rest of them. Oh God, what was that?"

Billy screamed, "Grenade! Hit the dirt!"

Then—bullets. Bullets—everywhere.

"Oh God! Now mortars! This is it! I hope it doesn't hurt. This is it!"

Booooooom! Booooooom! Artillery shells!

Billy yelled, "Incoming!"

"Oh God that's Billy's leg on me. Only Billy shined his boots like that. Where is the rest of him? I really liked Billy. I feel strangely at peace. That's weird! Oh God, don't let me die! I don't even know what to shoot at. Where are they? I don't want to die! I don't want to die! I don't want to die!"

Flash! Booooom! The earth shook beneath me, around me, over me. Dirt—everywhere.

"Why haven't I died yet?"

Bullets—bullets, everywhere—ike rain! Flashes! Explosions! Mortars! Death—death tugging at me—pulling me into the grave.

"Oh God. Oh my God—save me!"

Then the fire. Flames roaring. The heat—instant furnace!

"I can't breathe! I can't breathe! Why am I not on fire? I can't breathe!

I know hell! This is it! I feel at peace. That's weird. God—please!"

Then silence.

"Is this it? Am I dead? No."

The flames stopped. The bullets stopped. The noise stopped. I heard—bump bump—bump bump—bump bump.

"What is that?"

"My heart! I can hear my heart beating in my ears. I can't be dead—can I? Billy! Oh Billy. Where is everyone? Are they going to attack again? I should shout out to see if anyone else is alive. No, that would be stupid. Well, what do you know—I am still alive! Thank you God! I'm alive! Am I missing any parts? No. Are there any holes in me? No. My hair isn't even burned off. How can this be? Why me? Oh Thank you God. Stay quiet. The enemy is out there. I am alive! Thank you so much my dear, sweet God!"

"Did I yell that? No. Keep quiet, dummy. What a stupid worthless mission! Why didn't we stay back? Stupid! Stupid!"

An hour passed. Then two. Then three. No movement. No noise. No enemy. No friends. Just me laying there, looking up.

"Look at all those stars. How beautiful!"

"Are you out there God? Did you save me? You did save me! There is no possible way that I could have survived that attack! You did this! Why me?"

"What do I do now? How can I thank you for saving me? Do you want me to become a preacher or something? No way! That is not me, man. Tell me! Why don't you just come down here and tell me? What do I do now?"

I prayed, I cried, I rejoiced, I sulked, I grieved, I wept, I wept hard.

"I feel your presence, Father. I feel your power. I know your love. I

know complete acceptance. I know peace. I know hope. I've found a hunger for you. I know that I will never be the same again. I want to tell others. I want to tell everyone. I know that I will see you one day face to face. For now—we will be heart to heart. I am yours. You are mine."

"What a strange place to find God!"

"I better get out of here. I better get back to headquarters. I better tell those idiots!"

Years went by.

Now we are on to a new war. Everyone is still trying to forget the last war. I have often wondered if all this warring between people is just some kind of diversion. I have often wondered if many of the things that we focus on in our day to day lives are diversions. Tactics! A way to divert our attention away from the real battles.

Tactics are paramount to a successful war campaign. Get them focused on something else and then—baam! Blow 'em away. They didn't even see it comin'. A perfect ambush!

Satan is a master of war. He is a master of deceit. If he can keep us focused on the diversions of life, he can ambush us at will. Baam! We didn't even see him comin'.

The ultimate battle for us occurs between our ears. The battle for our allegiance. Who will we serve? Whose shall we be? We are born on the dark side.[1] We are also born with the gift of free will. The power of decision. The honor of choice.[2]

When we choose the light, we are free to stay in the light.

When we choose to stay in the darkness, we are slaves to the darkness. Bondage encompasses us. We will die the second death.[3]

We must choose.

Indecision is a choice.

We can turn our backs on the callings of the Father. We can reject the drawings of the Son. We can resist the pull of the Spirit. We can choose to ignore that still small voice within. That tender heart tug that lifts us toward the light. We can walk away. The decision is ours. The decision is ours alone.

We decide whose we are.

When the smoke clears, there will be one victor. When the battle for you is over, whose side will you stand on? Good or evil. Winner or loser?[4] Decide.

He willingly opens His arms spread wide with love and sends this message to you, "Come home."

Decide. Make a conscious decision. Examine the verdict that lies within you. Don't just loose by default, through indecision. Open the eyes of your heart. Listen to that still small voice within. You know that He has been calling you. Don't worry about your behavior, you can't change yourself anyway.[5] Don't believe that you are not good enough, none of us are, in our own right, but all of us can be, in Him.[6] Bring yourself home just the way you are now—He does the heart work.[7] Let His healing love pour down on you. Let His favor, His blessing, His desires pour over you. Let them soak in like a gentle rain, like a mist, like thick molasses. He longs for you to come home, like a grieving father longs for his estranged child to return.[8] Stop running. Stand still and listen.

Raise your vision beyond this tiny world. See the future. Don't be just another war casualty. Accept the victory that He has achieved for you. Stand in His presence—seek Him. Allow Him to become your Commander, He has won the war! Your battle may not be over yet, but victory has been achieved. Whose will you be?

Chapter Ten

The Perpetual Surrender

She meandered through the perfect portrait of beauty and design. Pastels in blues, purples, reds, yellows, oranges. Hues, shading toward wholeness. Somehow the fir and pine lined retreat brought a source of fullness. Symmetry! A voice that rejoiced with the brilliance of the Master Artist. The Creator's love on display. She loved this place and sought it out, especially in the springtime. Her sanctuary. She knew Him here. All the trials and tribulations of her personal conflicts were wiped away as she would strive to hike the three miles up that rocky slope, ascending toward her heavenly rendezvous, in the Creator's cathedral.

When she wearied of life's battles, her needy, hungry heart would pull her here. Here, amid the high country meadows. Here, where strife and chaos and clamor vanished more with each upward step. She had no decisions to make here. Somehow making the commitment to come eliminated every other choice. Here, her soul's voice harmonized with His. The vibrations of her searching heart echoed in unison with every pastel petal. The breeze whispered—love. The gentle brook, trickled and hummed as she smiled and released all to His care.

Sometimes she would weep. She would stretch out beside the crystal waters, beneath the warm blue canopy. She would absorb the soft life breathing rays of the tender morning sun and she would weep. Crying away every pain. Pouring out her struggle. Tears trickled down her flushed cheeks and washed away the battle. The hurt.

The Creator would bend low in those moments and hold her. He would draw her into His loving embrace and rock her sweetly while she wept. Perfect acceptance. Perfect peace. Complete release. *"Thank you for my tears, Daddy."* She would slumber, warmed by the gentle light of the Son. She would drift away on the clouds. Floating—higher and higher. Closer and closer toward home—toward heaven.

Revitalized she would reluctantly descend with the setting sun. Back down the mountain, back toward reality.

"Or was it unreality? Perhaps these sweet times with Him were the real reality. Why can't I just stay here? Constantly here. In my valley of peace."

His voice would echo in her heart. "I am with you always.[1] I will never leave you nor forsake you.[2] Neither death, nor life, nor shadow of darkness will separate you from my love."[3]

She knew it was true. She also knew herself, her history, her patterns, her habits. She would separate from Him, again and again. Even knowing that His sweet presence would be lost, she would still seek those dark paths. She would violate and tear apart their precious communion.

"Why?"

"It would just happen. One moment I am close to Him and fine. The next I am off on another dance with the darkness."

"Will I ever be free? Free to be free? Who am I? Whose am I?"

As she slowly crept down the hillside toward civilization, away from her valley of peace the storm raged in her heart. Those relentless, recurring questions assailed her mind.

"Who am I? Whose am I?"

She claimed to be His. But in those dark moments, she felt like she belonged to the enemy. She felt lost. But she liked this too. She enjoyed her perversions. She enjoyed her gossip. She enjoyed her over-powering appetites and passions. She knew that she sometimes worshiped them more than Him. She needed to come to a place where she could decide finally and forever—whose she was going to be.

"Who will I give my whole heart to? My love to? My soul to?"

"I will enter into a contract with Him—a covenant. I will write down my commitment to Him—that will do it! If it is written down and I sign it then I will not need to back track all the time. I will never again violate our tender relationship of faith, hope and love that I value so endearingly."

"It will be in writing. Solid! Unbreakable! An irreversible commitment! This will be it—no more will I choose the darkness!"

She found her car as she arrived at the trailhead. Jumping in, she slipped the key into the ignition, the engine roared, and she excitedly flew down the country roads toward home.

"I am ready to surrender all to You! I will put it in writing! I am yours! I am yours! If I put it in writing, it will be official."

Arriving at her house she rushed in. She found a clean, crisp sheet of brilliant white paper. As she contemplated it she pondered, *"I wish my soul were this clean."*

Then, that still small voice whispered once again its sweet refrain. "I have provided this for you. You are perfect, by faith in my gift.[4] I have blotted out your every transgression.[5] Your slate is clean."

Her eyes welled. A single tear began the torrent. The flood poured down her face, she sobbed a grateful river. *"How can You love me? How can You keep seeking me?"*

Then, the response, the answer that shook her heart to understanding. The light broke through the shadows.

His voice resounded. "My Darling child, I don't love you because of who you are. I love you because of who I am. I can be no other way. I want you so much that if you were the only person out of the billions of humans born into this brief, earthly battle that accepted my gift—I would have still come. If you were the only one, I would have still come. I would have come a billion times—for you. I would have laid down my royal crown, taken off my royal robes, left my dear Father's presence and risked it all for you. I would have paid the ransom for you alone. With me there is no shadow of turning. I am who I am.[6] I provided the power that grants you the freedom to choose." [7]

She cried back, "But, I don't seem to have the ability to do right. My character flaws keep bubbling up. I try to keep them under control, but I can't. I seem to always walk back down those dark ways. I get negative. I lust. I gossip. I hate. I cuss. I tear down. I turn my back on you, again and again."

"Stop!" His voice was loud and clear.

"Lift your eyes toward me. Reach out—reach up. It is all in your focus, your thoughts. You will rise or fall with your thoughts—your focus. By beholding you will become changed.[8] Feed your mind good food. Either your thoughts will enslave you, or by your thoughts you will be set free.[9] As a man thinks—so is he.[10] Let my mind become your mind.[11] If you put garbage in, you will get garbage out."

"Think about the diet that your mind is feeding upon. Negativity is the main course. Gossip, soap operas, crime shows, the daily news, the daily newspaper."

"Garbage in—garbage out."

"Feed your mind nourishing food.[12] Stay in the valley of peace. Remain in that place of hope. Rise above. Your desires will grow out of the diet you feed your mind."

"The conversion may be difficult for you. You may struggle with the change of menu. But begin. Change your hearts diet—now! Feed on me! Read about me! Look to me! Walk with me! Turn off the TV. Lay down the bad news. Focus on the good news. You may not be able to determine which thoughts enter your mind but you do have control of which ones that you play on its main screen. You do have a choice about what you feed your soul."

"This world is overflowing with wonderful, beautiful, uplifting experiences and activities. Seek them. Start now."

"I had my servants, the prophets of old record for you the human condition. The human hope. The Way up. This collection of dictated chronicles were written down for your benefit.[13, 14] Read them. Absorb them. Memorize, internalize, personalize them. They came at great cost. They are His story.[15] They are your story. Wars have been fought over them. Men have given their hearts, their souls, and their lives for them."

"They are the most published works in the world."

"Billions of souls have found in them—their home, their destiny. They are my love letters to you. The light from my heart shines through them."

"You dedicate hours sitting on your back side, staring hopelessly at the television, feeding your mind a steady diet of garbage. But you won't spend minutes feeding upon the good news contained in the message that I have sent to the earth—at great cost."

"Stop whining! You will reap what you sow.[16] As you plant the seeds of darkness into your soul—you will reap a harvest of black days. As you plant the seeds of light into your soul— you will reap a harvest of life and joy and love and peace and hope and power and victory and prosperity and usefulness and eternity."

"You will drink in the living water.[17] Your soul will be satisfied. Your dark desires will fall away as you walk in my presence. I am the Way, I am the Truth and I am the Life."[18]

"You have been given My very great and precious promises, through them you may participate in My divine nature. Through them you may escape the corruption that is in your heart caused by your own evil desires.[19] Feed upon and live out my promises."

"You must feed your body properly everyday for maximum physical health. You must feed your soul properly everyday for maximum spiritual health. Avoid unhealthy habits."

"Remember—this is not a one-time event. It is a meal that never ends. It is an ongoing, growing, enlarging experience, a continual heart surrender, an eternally expanding feast."

"Take your focus off of your seeming failure. Don't listen to the voice of discouragement, the voice of hopelessness, the voice of despair, the voice of defeat, the voice of the enemy. Keep your focus on the promises. The sure word of your Creator. I am your shepherd.[20] I am your valley of peace."

"I am the Way up—follow Me. You will seek Me and you will find Me, when you seek Me with all your heart."[21]

"All is yours. I sit on the throne. You are co-heir with me.[22] It becomes yours when you realize who you are. When you acknowledge whose you are. In my Father's house are many rooms—I have gone to prepare a place for you, that where I am, you may be also.[23] I paid your ransom. You are mine.

Look up. Open your mind. Open your hungry heart. Come to me."

"I willingly open my arms wide with love and send this message to you, 'Come home.'"

Chapter Eleven

The Force and the Victory

A gentle breeze drifted across His lifeless face. He had surpassed the end of His stored energy. Having hit the wall nearly two days before, He pushed on beyond the limits of what He had. Somewhere deep within Him, He found a drive, a force that compelled Him to continue striving to complete His combat assignment.

Alone—abandoned, He suffered the pangs of anxious apartness from everything human. There was only the Force that pushed Him. It was the Spirit that drove Him onward.[1] The humans He had walked the earth with did not comprehend His struggle. They didn't understand. No one understood, but the Father, the enemy and the Force. His task had to be accomplished or all would be lost. He longed for all to understand His mission—for all to understand that He had come to rescue them. He desired that all believe and accept the truth about His journey—His struggle. He was separated from the ones He had come to lift up, separated from them by their own volition. Knowing how desperately they needed what He came to deliver, He wept.

They were always listening to Him but never hearing, always watching Him but never seeing.[2] How could they be so dense? Like sheep—just dumb.[3] Wake up! He would cry in His soul. Wake up! It is not time to slumber. It is time to awaken.[4] The dawn is upon us. He would sigh and wish to be alone with the Force.

He had done something often during his travels among them. He would simply vanish. Disappear into the night.[5] He would allow the consciousness of His mission to slip away. He would allow the Force to envelope Him amidst the peaceful scenes of creation. He would commune with the Father and the Spirit. They would sooth His wounded humanness. They would encourage Him to move on to complete His vital task.

Nothing could stop Him from completing the mission of salvation, yet He would become frustrated at the slowness of those He was trying to reach. They couldn't see. They had no insights beyond their narrow vision of self.

He would shudder as the time approached for Him to become separated from the Father and the Spirit. He cringed as He knew that when He took upon himself the guilt of the whole world; the Father would not be able to stand in His presence. This loss was the only obstacle in His path. Suffering, He was accustomed to. Being ridiculed by His enemies, could not cause Him grief. But, being separated from the source of His every joy, His very essence. This He faced with deep reluctance.[6]

He knew that in giving Himself to face death, in giving Himself to be the bearer of the sins of all men, He would be torn from the Fathers presence. This is a separation they had never faced. This would create unfathomable emptiness, a void as large as all creation in the heart of the Father of love. I have wondered if His pain was not for Himself, but for those who would choose not to believe in his unending gift. His deepest regret may have been for the loss that the Father and the Spirit would endure, not only in losing the dearly-loved, rebellious angels of light and the children of earth, but also the thought of them suffering the loss of Him, if only for three short days, left Him numb, hollow, trembling with grief. He did not want anyone to suffer.[7]

The Father's great heart of love was saddened at the loss of Lucifer. He was saddened at the loss of a third of the Heavenly angels of light. He was saddened at the loss of many, many, many of the children of earth.[8] All of this grieved the Father's wounded, breaking heart, but when the Son of God would willingly take upon himself the entire weight and burden of sin, the Father would lose his Son. The express image of all that He is, would die. His Son would forever bear marks of that day.[9]

The Creator of all the universe would lay it all down and willingly be crushed to death by the sadness His Father would endure.[10, 11] For love does not consider self. Love is defined through complete and unreserved giving of all that one has, of all that one is. There is no greater love than to lay down your life for your friends.[12]

The breeze had stopped. It seemed that now there was only the scorching sun. His dominant sensation was the rawness in His parched, baked throat.

His weakness, His exhaustion was complete. He had gone to the end of every breath that His humanness had to bring. He had been forty days without a meal, alone, in the desert of testing.[13] Alone except for the Force inside Him and the enemy that had come to torment and to tempt Him.[14] For if the enemy could cause Him to violate the mere essence of the laws of love; if he could cause the Creator to concede to even as much as a doubt, he might be victorious and the war might not be over. Evil might not be vanquished. The story that you know so well might have a different ending. There might be no happily ever after, no hope for a bright and glorious future. The darkness might penetrate the universe until chaos overwhelmed it.

The Father would allow this test. All beings throughout the cosmos would watch as the Son of God would subject Himself to the test of allegiance. In the most tortuous scenario possible the enemy would be allowed to launch his cunning attacks upon God's Son. All intelligent beings were focused on this stage. Should their Creator fail, the war might never end. But He would not fail. The possibility existed. It could happen. But there would be no failure. The Father had allowed His own Son to humble Himself and assume the frailty of humanness and entrusted Him with the hope of all.

This would be the beginning of the end of Satan and his attacks upon the laws of love and upon the Father's government. He attacked the Creator in the same ways that he attacks us. His weapons of war are deceit, doubt and worship of other gods.[16]

These are the life-ending tools he used to pry the angels of light and uses to seduce the children of earth away from their allegiance to the Father.

He would use them again on this exhausted, starving and weakened survivor.

But he could not and cannot break through the fortress of faith. He could not overcome the heart of love.

Love is the power that energizes all of the Father's vast enterprise. Love is a force. This is the Force that pushed the Son of God on. This is the Force that ignited in Him the strength to overcome the temptations of Satan.

This power is ours.[17] We obtain it through the surrender of self and faith in His power, merits and victories.

When the Son of God completed His mission upon our

troubled planet He united Himself with the brotherhood of man by a tie that will never be broken. Throughout all eternity He will be identified with us—with humanity. When all is concluded, when the Father, the Son and the Spirit gather on that day—that day when the lake of fire will consume this section of the universe. When all who have chosen by their own free will, not to be a part of the kingdom of light, are given their way out through the second death.[18] The Father, the Son and the Spirit will create a new heaven and a new earth.[19] We will dwell there with them and the loyal angels of light, eternally.[20]

He places in all who accept His offering, the essence of Himself.[21] He elevates us to a height above all that we could possibly dream or imagine. We are co-heirs with Him.[22] We are now and forever more—blood brothers. All power has been given to Him.[23] We have free and total access to His power. It is ours—freely granted by grace. We have been set free.[24] Because of His sacrifice, we stand no longer under the tragic results of our rebellion from the law, but under grace—we are pardoned. He has ensured our calling and election into the kingdom of light.

The hope of perfect bliss, perfect peace, perfect obedience, perfect happiness and perfect health are all ours. No disease, no loss, no tears, no pain, no lack, no want, no sorrow, no grief, no separation, no anxiety. These are the benefits, the natural consequences of living under the laws of love. These are ours.

This is free grace—a gift.[25]

When you were a child and someone gave you a toy or a piece of candy or a meal—anything, you simply accepted it as yours. Then you would fight for it if anyone else tried to take it away. This salvation is the greatest gift of all. The Father offers it freely to us. Take it. Fight for it. Don't let anyone, especially an already defeated enemy, take your gift from you—fight the good fight of faith.[26]

Awaken!

Stop turning a deaf ear to His voice that calls you.[27] Seek the light. You know when you do and you know when you don't.

Look inside yourself. He is there. The kingdom of the Father is inside you.[28] He is out there trying to get in, and He is in you trying to get out. As you open the channel - His love, His peace and His service will begin to flow through you as a trickle begins. This trickle, if fed, will become a stream, then a river of life, flowing out to all, bringing living water to the thirsty.[29]

Don't be a dead sea. Don't be a hole where living water flows in but doesn't flow out. Don't be a sink hole of putrid greed that only receives and never gives. It is in giving that we are blessed. It is better to give than to receive.

With the cup you use to distribute your blessings to others it will be distributed back to you.[30] A generous man will himself be blessed.[31]

The heart of love gives.

During the last night of His deadly mission on earth, His humanness shrank at the challenge He faced. He had walked once again to His garden retreat. Only this time His steps were heavy with hesitation. His human followers had drifted off to sleep. Alone, once again, He pleaded with the Father. Let this cup of woe pass! Three times he begged that there could be some other way. But there was not. The only hope for mankind was to be rescued by the Father, the Son and the Spirit. Three times while sweating great drops of blood He withdrew from the task. His human side and His great heart of love did not want to endure the separation from the Father and the Spirit. He did not want to endure death. He did not want the Father and the Spirit to feel that pain.

But love knows no other way. love saves, love gives, love obeys. Satan was there, feeding Him his round of lies, hoping for Him to give up, hoping for Him to walk away.

Then—the surrender. Not My will, but your will be done, Father.[32, 33]

Satan knew that it was over. Once the decision was made—he was defeated. This moment was the defining victory in the war between good and evil. His decision.

The decision He made in that moment set us free. It released all creation from the threat of war. It preserved inviolate those who choose the Way of love. It gave hope to all creation. This decision, you and I must make also; to do the will of the Father or the will of Satan. Know this—there is no middle ground. You may wish to deny it. You may wish to ignore it. You may wish to sedate it. You may wish to serve another. But decide you will.

Indecision is a decision.

His decision was supported by His actions. Within moments of His surrender He was rushed off by a maddened crowd. He was subjected to the worst kind of humiliation and torture. It was difficult—it was joyful. It was filled with blinding pain, ripped and torn flesh, ridicule, scorn, hope, faith, love, giving, rejoicing and grieving for those who would walk away from the single greatest gift the universe has ever known.[34]

It was a display of cruelty that would reveal the true heart of Satan, the enemy of right. But the real battle had been won the night before, in the valley of decision. This is where the war is fought. It is fought in our hearts and minds. It is fought in the core of our soul. The place where we decide who we are. The place where we decide whose we are. You know this place. You know this struggle.

His decision led to His complete submission to the benevolent will of our Father. It led to a hill called—the place of the skull. It was a victory walk for us. It led to him being nailed to a tree. On this tree he spread open His arms wide with love and sent this message to all, "Come home."

Chapter Twelve

Whose Are You?

The party was over now. He had been unable to sleep because the grown-ups party had been so loud outside his door. For hours he lay there hoping that tonight would be different. Wishing that Mom and Dad would come into his bedroom and give him a gentle, loving embrace and a good night kiss, instead of—you know—the drunken screaming, the yelling, the sound of glasses and plates shattering as she would throw them at him—the painful sounds of flesh pounding flesh as he would strike her in brutal anger.

But tonight wasn't different. He could hear the muffled beginnings of the battle through his closed door. He would retreat to the corner of the room and turn on the little space heater in an attempt to drown out the sounds, those horrible, heart wrenching, tear evoking sounds. He would try to get lost in the soft warm breeze that would pour forth from the heater. Somehow it would comfort him. He didn't know why but lying in front of that little heater, listening to its gentle whir, feeling the warm air caress his face, his soul, he felt safe. He tried to disappear.

She was screaming now, and cursing him. Get off me you son-of-a-#@#!@.

Then—his Dad's mean voice and the heart-breaking sounds of his fist striking her face.

The shattered child's little heart pounded against his small chest. Fear gripped him. Confusion. Terror. Tears and trembling. He cried, "Please stop! Please Stop! Please stop!"

He held his hands over his ears and pushed his face closer to the heater—closer to his place of comfort—his place of safety.

She was trying to get away. He could hear her run toward the front door—she didn't make it.

More screaming, cursing, furniture being slammed against the wall.

Then, He would come. His presence would drift into the room. He would bend low and place His arms around the shaking, timid little boy and hold him close to His chest. He would not say a word. He would simply hold him and rock. His sweet, gentle, loving touch brought solace to the young boy's bewildered heart. There was peace, love, security, safety, hope. The tears would stop. He never saw His face. He was more like a presence than a human, but He was real. He was a different kind of being. love-based. He didn't need to open the door to come in. He would just be there. He would be there when it got really bad. The small child knew that His name was Jesus. He didn't know why he knew that His name was Jesus, he just knew it. He had heard that name before, but only in the context of cursing. He knew nothing about Him, except His love, His peace, His tender presence.

The whimpering child would feel calmness come over his soul as Jesus would comfort and sooth his fearful, tearful heart. Slumber would come upon him and a sweet, peaceful sleep would carry him away.

The little boy knew that he belonged to Jesus. He knew that Jesus would come to take him home one day. He had been given a sharp, clear, impressive dream one night. It was vivid and real, a prophecy, a future event. The small child had never seen or heard of anything like this. In his dream he was coming up out of the earth. He was floating up, rising into the sky. He was a spirit. He was not in human flesh, but it was him. There were others also. They were rising into the air with Him, going up into the sky. There was a girl coming out of the grave next to his. He knew her and he loved her but he didn't know her name.

As he rose into the sky he passed by Jesus. Jesus was sitting on a throne that rested on a cloud. He had a crown upon His head. He was dressed in royal robes. He had something in His right hand. His face was sad. Then it was over.

This vision would comfort the young boy. He knew that he belonged to Jesus, even though as he grew he would try to deny it. He would live a life away from Him. He would violate the laws of love deliberately and blatantly. He would deny the existence of the Father, the Son and the Spirit. He would preach that there was no God. He would walk down that dark empty path toward a fruitless life of debauchery and death. Lying, stealing, adultery—whatever felt good at the time.

Running, hiding, hurting, he flew through life not caring about anyone but himself. From time to time he would wake up in strange places, with strange people, in strange cars, in airports, in fields, in snow banks, in jails, in suffering, in pain—always pain. Not simply the pain suffered from chemical abuse but the pain of emptiness, the pain of sorrow, the pain of loss. He suffered deeply.

Yet back in his mind and down in his heart he couldn't shake the drawing, the incessant calling for his soul, the inner voice that he tried to deny—to push down—to run from—to sedate.

Do you hear that voice also—or have you been successful in shutting it off? Hopefully not.

He tired of the emptiness of his worldly lifestyle. He would seek the Father, the Son and the Spirit. He would find Jesus. He would go to church and be a good little boy. What a disappointment. Not only was the church full of other bad little boys and girls but he found that he couldn't be good. The dark side had a grip on him and would not let go. His heart still wanted to re-capture the good times of the past. He would seek them again. He would find them just as empty as before.

He would flail about like a fish on dry land. No place to call home. He couldn't go back. That life was too painful. He needed help. He would get a Bible and read it for himself. Somehow he knew that his hope was to be found in the words of that book. But he couldn't understand it. He didn't find hope in there. He found death, lust, debauchery, murder, war. The human condition. He couldn't get it. He would throw it against the wall. He hated it. He threw it against the wall until it fell apart. He felt hopeless.

He found himself in a Revelation Seminar. The speaker, Leon, was a bright, inspiring, county boy from Idaho. He explained the words of the Father in power and in truth. It finally all made sense. All of the confusion was cleared away. These people actually read and understood this book. There was a slide show that accompanied Leon's presentation. Toward the end of the seminar it happened! There it was—his childhood vision! His dream! The resurrection day experience that he was given so early in life. There He was exactly as he had seen Him. Sitting on a throne on a cloud, a crown on His head, something in His right hand, a sad face. It was exactly as he had seen it so many years before. Exactly! It was Jesus—our Creator![1]

He knew that he belonged to Jesus. He was home. All was forgiven. All hope returned. There was fullness. Completeness. He knew whose he was. He was drawn into the hearts of those gentle, truth bearing souls. He joined them and still worships with that same little church family. He still studies with those people regularly, on the Sabbath Day.

He would like you to also discover—whose you are.

The Father would like you to know—whose you are.

You may want to understand—whose you are. You are an heir to the throne! By faith in the gift!

If you really want to know whose you are, you may wish to get yourself a copy of the most enlightened, most published, most sought after, most fought over collection of writings this world has ever or will ever know—*The Holy Scriptures.* Many Bible scholars agree that the most accurate translation of the original scriptures is the *New American Standard Bible.* If you want a place to start or enhance your study of the Scriptures then
please read all of the verses that are listed in the Quotations/ Paraphrases section of this book.

There are many, many beautiful books describing the Passion of our Creator and Savior. You may enjoy some of our other books which are described in the back of this one.

Find a family of folks that study and search the scriptures. Join them as they strive together to discover and surrender to the will of the Father.

Seek Him in His word. Seek Him in the company of others. Also seek Him in His creation. Spend time with Him in His natural world, outside of man-made environments. You will find Him there as well.

But mostly seek Him in your own heart. He is there—waiting.

When your brief journey on planet earth is over, you will belong to the darkness or to the light. The choice is yours. We hope you choose the light.

He is calling.

He willingly spreads His arms wide with love and sends this message to you, "Come home."

Promises

I have often awakened me in the deep of the night. While sleeping soundly, dreaming my little dreams, suddenly—He has come to me. His words vibrating in my soul, "I have an undercover mission, a matter of universal interest. I want you to use your voice to share my love with others."

He prepared me for this time. All of my experience in the war between good and evil has been a training ground for this mission. When He calls, I rise from my slumber and sit—listening. Waiting for inspiration. Ready to take dictation. Then He enlightens my mind with His thoughts, His words, His vision for you and for me. Urgent messages for all who have ears to hear. He wants us to catch a glimpse of what is in store for those who choose him. *The Holy Scriptures* are packaged in promise. All of the Father's promises are ours, in the gift of His willing sacrifice for us, in His Son—Jesus Christ.

These are some of the rights, gifts and privileges of those who accept and obey Him. The benefits of being adopted into the royal family.

His sure promises include eternal life,[1] freedom from slavery to a defective character,[2] joy, patience, kindness, goodness, gentleness, faithfulness, self-control, love, peace, faith, hope[3] and His boundless favor.[4]

Everything you touch will prosper.[5]

You will be the head and not the tail. You will be blessed when you go in and blessed when you go out. You will be blessed in the country and you will be blessed in the city. Your enemies will flee from you.[6] You will have victory over self.[7] He will create in you a new heart.[8] He will write His laws on your heart and on your mind.[9] Purity of thought and action are yours.[10] You shall not want.[11] You shall have a shepherd to watch over you and protect you.[12] He will be your fortress, your shield, your stronghold, your strength, your rock.[13] You will be in good heath and prosper.[14] He will never leave you or abandon you.[15] He will give you abundant life.[16] He will restore your soul. He will set a table for you in the presence of your enemies. Your cup will overflow. Goodness and love will chase you down and overtake you. You will dwell in the house of the Father, forever.[17]

You will know a future beyond your short span of years here on planet earth.[18] You will seek Him and you will find Him, when you seek Him with all of your heart.[19]

His Spirit will dwell in you, guiding you, directing your steps.[20] His word will be a light on your path.[21] Super-natural blessings will come upon you.[22]

In this world you will also have trouble, but be cheerful for he has overcome the world. You will know peace in the midst of trials.[23] The trials you experience are allowed to come upon you to assist in molding your character into His.[24] The Father will discipline the children that He loves.[25]

Everything you need for life, here and hereafter is yours.[26]

His favor and His blessings will pour down upon you like rain, like a soaking, like a heavy spring dew, like sweet molasses, covering and protecting you.

Even though you walk through the valley of the shadow of death you will fear no evil for He is with you. His rod and his staff will comfort you.[27]

You will reap what you sow.[28]

The precious gift of free will is yours, the choice is yours.[29] All of these benefits, rights and privileges are yours if you choose to accept His free gift of adoption into the Father's family and obey the great laws of love.[30] These royal rights and gifts are yours as well as many, many, many more. So many promises, and benefits, and gifts are yours that it will take eternity to discover them all.

The Father's laws are right and just and true. They will never be changed.[31] They will be upheld. The consequence of abandoning the laws of His government is death. But His gift to you is life.[32] Your violations of the laws of love have been cast into the farthest depths of the ocean.[33] They are as far away as the east is from the west.[34] He is your sin bearer. He has paid your ransom.[35] You are free! If you choose to be free.[36]

Once this dark story is over, there will never again be any being that wishes to usurp the Father's government. We will know the results of choosing to stray from the perfect laws of love. We will desire only the best for ourselves as well as any and all other beings. We delight in doing His will for we know that it is the very best that can ever be.[37]

Jesus is the Way, the Truth and the Life.[38]

Come home to Him. His great heart of love has given all for you.

Trust in the Lord with all your heart and lean not on your own understanding. In all your ways acknowledge Him and He will make your paths straight.[39]

We hope that you have chosen to walk with us as we strive to know and to follow the Way up. The Way back home to our happy beginnings. Our greatest longing is to travel deep into the outer reaches of this vast ever-expanding universe and continually discover it's incredibly awe-inspiring treasures with the Father, the Son, the Spirit and you.

—*James Bars*

Quotations and Paraphrases

The words of this book were inspired by the Spirit. The Bible verses, footnoted in each chapter are listed below. The verses from each chapter are either in the form of direct quotation, paraphrase or summation.

NIV – *New International Version*

TNIV – *The New International Version*

CHAPTER 2
[1] Ephesians 1:18 NIV
[2] Revelation 3:2-3 NIV
[3] Job 38:19 NIV

CHAPTER 3
[1] Job 38:19 NIV
[2] 1 John 1:5 & 1 John 4:16 NIV
[3] Genesis 2:8 NIV
[4] Revelation 21:21 NIV
[5] Hebrews 1:13 NIV
[6] Proverbs 2:1-6 NIV
[7] Matthew 16:19 NIV
[8] John 8:32 NIV
[9] Matthew 11:15 NIV
[10] Psalm 50:16-22 NIV
[11] Revelation 20:11-15 NIV
[12] John 14:27 NIV

CHAPTER 4
[1] John 10:10 NIV
[2] Isaiah 14:12 NIV
[3] Ezekiel 28:14-15 NIV
[4] Isaiah 14:13-14 NIV
[5] Ezekiel 28 16-19 NIV

[6] 1 John 3:8 NIV
[7] Colossians 2:11-15 NIV
[8] Hebrews 2:14-18 NIV
[9] 1 Corinthians 13:8 NIV
[10] Jeremiah 17:9 NIV

CHAPTER 5
[1] Genesis 3:1-13 NIV
[2] Romans 6:23 NIV
[3] Romans 8:22-23 NIV
[4] Genesis 3:4-5 NIV
[5] Revelation 12:7-9 NIV
[6] Genesis 3:7-10 NIV

CHAPTER 6
[1] Genesis 1:1-2 NIV
[2] Colossians 1:15-23 NIV
[3] Colossians 3:5-11 NIV
[4] Genesis 1:3 -2:25 NIV
[5] Romans 1:20 NIV
[6] Genesis 1:26 NIV
[7] Genesis 3:1 NIV
[8] Genesis 2:16-17 NIV
[9] Genesis 3:2-3 NIV
[10] Genesis 3:21-24 NIV

[11] Genesis 3:1-7 NIV
[12] Genesis 2:15-17 NIV
[13] Romans 7:21-26 NIV
[14] John 1:1-4 NIV
[15] Romans 7:21-25 NIV

CHAPTER 7

[1] Revelation 20:13-15 NIV
[2] Matthew 16:19 NIV
[3] John 15:5 NIV
[4] John 19:30 NIV
[5] Hebrews 12:1-6 NIV
[6] John 15:1-11 NIV
[7] Romans 6:23 NIV
[8] Hebrews 9:11-10:18 NIV
[9] 1 John 2:1-6 NIV
[10] John 15:12-14 NIV
[11] Matthew 27:45-54 NIV

CHAPTER 8

[1] Revelation 12:1-17 NIV
[2] Revelation 20: 7-15 NIV
[3] 2 Thessalonians 2:8-12 NIV
[4] 2 Peter 3:8-9 NIV
[5] John 10:7-10 NIV
[6] Genesis 4:1-12 NIV
[7] 2 Timothy 3:1-9 NIV
[8] Romans 8:22 NIV
[9] Galatians 5:19-21 NIV
[10] Galatians 5:22-26 NIV
[11] Jeremiah 29:11-14 NIV
[12] Romans 12:1-2 NIV
[13] Genesis 3:14-15 NIV
[14] 2 Thessalonians 2:1-12 NIV
[15] John 8:44 NIV
[16] Hebrews 11:1 NIV
[17] Matthew 17:20-21 NIV

[18] Ephesians 2:8-10 NIV
[19] Hebrews 11:6 NIV
[20] Romans 10:17 NIV
[21] Luke 1:26-38 NIV
[22] Luke 3:21-23 NIV
[23] Hebrews 4:15 NIV
[24] 1 Corinthians 7:23 NIV
[25] Matthew 27:32-54 NIV
[26] Matthew 28:11 NIV
[27] Revelation 20:6 NIV
[28] 1 Corinthians 15:50-58 NIV
[29] Galatians 2:15-3:29 NIV

CHAPTER 9

[1] Romans 5:12-21 NIV
[2] Romans 6:15-23 NIV
[3] Revelation 20:11-15 NIV
[4] Revelation 21:1-8 NIV
[5] Romans 7:14-8:17 NIV
[6] Romans 3:21-26 NIV
[7] Philippians 1:3-6 NIV
[8] Luke 15:11-32 NIV

CHAPTER 10

[1] Matthew 28:18-20 TNIV
[2] Joshua 1:5 TNIV
[3] Romans 8:31-39 TNIV
[4] Galatians 2:15-21 TNIV
[5] Isaiah 43:25 TNIV
[6] Exodus 3:13 TNIV
[7] Ephesians 3:14-21 TNIV
[8] Hebrews 12:1-3 TNIV
[9] Mark 7:14-23 TNIV
[10] Matthew 22:37-40 TNIV
[11] Romans 12:1-2 TNIV
[12] Philippians 4:4-9 TNIV
[13] 2 Timothy 3:16-17 TNIV

[14] 2 Peter 1:20-21 TNIV

[15] John 5:39-40 TNIV

[16] Galatians 6:7 TNIV

[17] Revelation 21:6-7 TNIV

[18] John 14:6 TNIV

[19] 2 Peter 1:3-11 TNIV

[20] John 10:11-18 TNIV

[21] Jeremiah 29:13 TNIV

[22] Romans 8:12-17 TNIV

[23] John 14:1-3 TNIV

CHAPTER 11

[1] Luke 4:1-2 TNIV

[2] Matthew 13:10-23 TNIV

[3] 1 Peter 2:24-25 TNIV

[4] Ephesians 5:12-18 TNIV

[5] Luke 22:39 TNIV

[6] Luke 22:40-44 TNIV

[7] Mark 14:32-36 TNIV

[8] Revelation 12:3-17 TNIV

[9] John 20:24-31 TNIV

[10] John 1:1-3 TNIV

[11] Colossians 1:15-23 TNIV

[12] John 15:12-17 TNIV

[13] Luke 4:1-2 TNIV

[14] Luke 4:3-13 TNIV

[16] Luke 4:3-13 TNIV

[17] Ephesians 1:15-23 TNIV

[18] Revelation 20:7-15 TNIV

[19] Revelation 21:1 TNIV

[20] Revelation 21:2-27 TNIV

[21] 2 Corinthians 1:21-22 TNIV

[22] Romans 8:16-17 TNIV

[23] John 13:3 TNIV

[24] Galatians 5:1 TNIV

[25] Revelation 21:3-7 TNIV

[26] 1Timothy 1:18-19 TNIV

[27] 1 Kings 19:11-13 TNIV

[28] Luke 17:20-21 TNIV

[29] John 7:37-38 TNIV

[30] Luke 6:38 TNIV

[31] Proverbs 22:9 TNIV

[32] Matthew 26:36-46 TNIV

[33] Luke 22:39-46 TNIV

[34] Luke 22:47-23:56 TNIV

CHAPTER 12

[1] Revelation 20:11 TNIV

EPILOGUE

[1] John 3:15-21 TNIV

[2] Galatians 5:1 TNIV

[3] Galatians 5:19-26 TNIV

[4] Luke 4:18-19 TNIV

[5] Deuteronomy 30:9-10 TNIV

[6] Deuteronomy Ch. 28 TNIV

[7] Matthew 10:39 TNIV

[8] Ezekiel 36:25-27 TNIV

[9] Jeremiah 31:33 TNIV

[10] Philippians 4:8 TNIV

[11] Psalm 23:1 TNIV

[12] John 10:11-18 TNIV

[13] Psalm 18:1-2 TNIV

[14] 3 John 2 TNIV

[15] John 14:15-21 TNIV

[16] John 10:10 TNIV

[17] Psalm 23 TNIV

[18] John 17:3 TNIV

[19] Jeremiah 29:11-14 TNIV

[20] John 14:15-21 TNIV

[21] Psalm 119:105 TNIV

[22] Matthew 5:3-12 TNIV

[23] John 16:33 TNIV

24 James 1:2-8) TNIV
25 Hebrews 12:7-13 TNIV
26 2 Peter 1:3-11 TNIV
27 Psalm 23:4 TNIV
28 Galatians 6:7 TNIV
29 Joshua 24:14-15 TNIV
30 Romans 8:23 TNIV
31 Mark 13:31 TNIV
32 Romans 6:23 TNIV
33 Micah 7:18-19 TNIV
34 Psalm 103:8-14 TNIV
35 1 John 2:1-2 TNIV
36 2 Corinthians 3:7-4:6 TNIV
37 Psalm 119:44-48 TNIV
38 John 14:6 TNIV
39 Proverbs 3:5-6

GOD, PLEASE REWIRE MY MADFATs

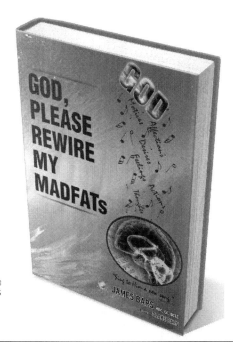

 JAMES BARS, BCC, CCLC
Co-author, **BLAKE BARS**

The Ultimate Treasure Chest For Love-based Living:

* God's Holy Spirit will rewire and ignite within you, inspiring, joy-filled Motives, Affections, Desires, Feelings, Actions and Thoughts—MADFATs.

* Your heart will feast on the riches of eternal wisdom, knowledge and understanding.

* You will mine the depths of advanced mind renewal emerging transformed and wealthy beyond all earthly treasure.

* You will rightly combine neuroscience, Scripture and the Holy Spirit's power with a system for success that will enrich your physical, mental, emotional and spiritual well-being.

* You will possess a clearer vision of your purpose and your soul's restoration.

* You will experience a liberating journey into the unending fortunes that are yours as a cherished member of the family of God. Yay!

ISBN: 978-0-9817534-3-0
$14.95

available at
MyNewMADFATs.com

Recovery Journal

A Journal is defined as:
A personal record of experiences and reflections.

A Journey is defined as:
A passage from one place to another.

This book is both.

 **JAMES BARS**

This fun and enlightening book is an uplifting, light-bearing companion that will assist in expanding and adding color to the horizons in your mind.

You will laugh out loud.

You will open previously barricaded gardens in your soul.

You will discover the Kingdom of God that lies within you.

You will dispel the darkness that has bound you in slavery.

You will be Happy, Joyous and Free!

Enjoy this Journal and this Journey, with God.

ISBN: 978-0-9862397-2-4
$14.95

available at
MyNewMADFATs.com

Exposing God

Amidst the Chaos

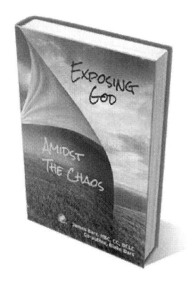

Is God fair?
Is He loving?
Would a fair and loving God take His sick child and eternally torture that child for being born sick? This is the current view of God now portrayed to the world.
Could our perception of God be wrong?
Let's pull back the curtain and take a closer look at our God of love.

IF YOU ARE AFRAID OF GOD, SOMEONE HAS BEEN LYING TO YOU.

This is an excellent book for souls who have been damaged by fear-based perceptions of God.

Book Price $5.99
ISBN: 978-0-9862397-0-0

 JAMES BARS, BCC, CELC
Co-author, BLAKE BARS

available at
MyNewMADFATs.com

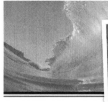

Your Own Christian Counselor and Master Life Coach

James Bars – Christian Counselor,
Board Certified Master Life Coach,
Human Behavior Consultant, Author

Are you... Stuck? Hurting? Broken? Burnt out? Addicted? Changing? Powerless?

In need of... Conflict Resolution! Freedom! Purpose! Balance! Direction! Fulfillment!

Explore our: *Your Inner Counselor - A Holy Spirit
Guided Problem Resolution Process*

*We are delighted to offer clarifying, effective,
Christ-centered resources and services.*

Our goal is your everlasting success!

Access our: *Coaching/Counseling Services.*

Marriage/Relationship	Finances
Goal Setting/Accomplishment	Career/Personal Mentoring
Mid-life Crisis/Aging Concerns	Depression/Anxiety
Parenting/Blended Family Issues	Conflict/Anger Management
Addictions/Eating Disorders	Grief/Loss
Self-worth	Health/Wellness

---

*Contact Us For Christian
Counseling & Coaching*

Email: MyNewMADFATs@gmail.com
On the web: MyNewMADFATs.com

Live Free, Love Right, Dispel the Darkness, Know the Light

Made in the USA
San Bernardino, CA
30 November 2015